Derbyshire Railways

on old picture postcards

Brian Lund

1. Derby Midland Railway station opened on 11th May 1840 when the North Midland Railway commenced running trains to Masborough. At the same time, two earlier stations – one owned by the Midland Counties Railway, and the other by the Birmingham and Derby Junction Railway – were closed, and their services diverted to the new station. All three companies combined to form the Midland Railway on 10th May 1844. Derby became the focal point of the company's network, with services operating to locations as far apart as Bournemouth and Glasgow. The station was extended in 1881, and the platform extensively rebuilt in 1954 following wartime bomb damage. The exterior has been modernised in recent years. This postcard by Valentine of Dundee shows a busy interior scene about 1908.

ISBN 0 946245 86 X

£3.50

Reprinted or revised 1997, 1998, 1999

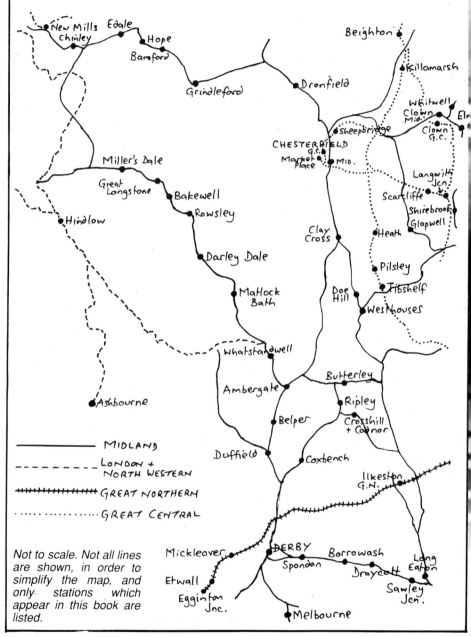

Derbyshire railway stations featured in this book, with pre-grouping (1923) lines indicated

New Mills
Chinley
Edale
Hope
Bamford
Grindleford
Dronfield
Beighton
Killamarsh
Whitwell
Clown Mid.
Elm
Clown G.C.
Sheepbridge
CHESTERFIELD
Market Place
G.C.
MID.
Miller's Dale
Great Longstone
Bakewell
Rowsley
Langwith Jcn.
Scarcliffe
Shirebrook
Glapwell
Hindlow
Darley Dale
Clay Cross
Heath
Pilsley
Tibshelf
Doe Hill
Westhouses
Matlock Bath
Whatstandwell
Butterley
Ambergate
Ripley
Crosshill + Codnor
Ashbourne
Belper
Duffield
Coxbench
Ilkeston G.N.

MIDLAND
LONDON + NORTH WESTERN
GREAT NORTHERN
GREAT CENTRAL

Not to scale. Not all lines are shown, in order to simplify the map, and only stations which appear in this book are listed.

Mickleover
Etwall
Egginton Jnc.
DERBY
Spondon
Melbourne
Borrowash
Draycott
Long Eaton
Sawley Jcn.

Published June 1995. Reprinted or revised 1997, 1998, 1999

2. Spondon, on the Midland line to Nottingham, was opened in 1839. Goods traffic ceased in 1965, but the station still provides a passenger service. A bay platform, to the left of the near one, was opened in 1918 for workmen's services to and from the Celanese factory.

BORROWASH STATION.

3. Borrowash, the next station on the line, had 14 passenger stopping train services each way on weekdays in 1910, with four on Sundays. It closed in February 1966. This particular station opened in 1871, replacing the original 1839 one situated to the east of the road bridge.

INTRODUCTION

The coming of the railways in the nineteenth century revolutionised social life, bringing speed and efficiency to the delivery and transport of all kinds of goods, milk and dairy produce, mail and newspapers. Opportunities for personal travel were immediately widened, though this benefit only filtered through gradually to all sections of society.

If the railway system of Britain had been centrally planned and better organised, it might have become more prosperous and lasted longer. But different lines were built by competing individual companies and privately-funded, and rivalry often meant duplication of routes. Stations, especially village ones, were often inconveniently situated because of problems of geography, cost, or local landowner opposition. Sometimes stations were built to serve two communities and sited in between, with difficult access for both.

Derbyshire was dominated from the start by the Midland Railway, which in 1844 took over routes already initiated, and enlarged a network covering much of the county. Derby was the hub of the company's operations, on the north-south main line. The prestigious route through the Peak District gave the Midland access to the north-west and was heavily advertised in company promotion.

Many other companies were involved in railway building in the county, often primarily to transport goods rather than passengers: Derbyshire's industrial and railway histories are closely linked in the nineteenth century. By 1910, take-overs of the smaller concerns meant that the Midland, Great Northern, Great Central and London & North-Western companies controlled the county's network, with a brief incursion by the North Staffordshire to Ashbourne.

In 1923 most railways were placed into four main groups, two of which directly affected Derbyshire. These were the London, Midland & Scottish, and the London and North Eastern. Competition from road traffic began to threaten the railways by the 1930s, and the heavy toll taken of the system during the Second World War also led to pressure to cut costs by closures after nationalisation in 1947. Most closures occurred in the 1960's.

This book is not intended to be a history of railway stations in Derbyshire, but a selection of pictures giving a flavour of the Golden Age of Railways. If I haven't included your favourite station, apologies – perhaps a second volume will be viable in the future! The choice of illustrations was governed by which postcards were available.

The boom years for picture postcards were from 1902-14, co-inciding with a halcyon period for rail travel. Cards of stations, particularly the small local ones, are difficult to find, and because the postcard collector is competing with the railway enthusiast they have become expensive. Cards of the larger town and city stations were published by major national firms like W.H. Smith (whose cards often featured their own news-stands) but coverage of village stations was haphazard, depending on a keen local photographer. Publishers are mentioned in the captions where known.

Back cover (top): **Hindlow**, on the L.N.W.R. line from Ashbourne to Buxton. Most of the stations on this route served very small communities, and goods traffic provided the main revenue. Hindlow closed in 1954, at the same time as Ashbourne. Much of the line south of the station has been converted by Derbyshire County Council to a footpath/cycleway.

(bottom): **Grindleford**, on the Sheffield-Manchester Hope Valley Line *(see illus. 32).*

Acknowledgements: illustrations 2-5, 7-9, 11, 13-14, 16-22, 24-34, 40-41, 44, 49-50 reproduced courtesy Lens of Sutton; nos. 6, 12, 23, 35-39, 42-43, 45-47, 51-54 courtesy of Alan Bower; no.10 courtesy of David Limer. I should also like to thank Glynn Waite and Alan Rimmer for advice and assistance with certain details of railway history. Any inaccuracies are entirely my own responsibility.

4. Draycott and Breaston also lost its passenger service in 1966, as bus traffic slowly eroded customer usage. It was opened as Draycott in 1852; Breaston was not added until 1939.

5. Sawley Junction, opened in 1888, was one of the important stations on the line which has survived to the present day. It was renamed Long Eaton in 1968, the fourth station in the vicinity to be given that name!

6. Long Eaton station on the Erewash Valley Line between Trent and Clay Cross, seen on a 'Peveril' series postcard c.1908. It closed to passengers in January 1967.

7. Melbourne station seen on a card published by E. Martin, was on a Midland line connecting Ashby-de-la-Zouch with Derby. Even at the height of the railway's importance, only six trains a day stopped in each direction, and services ceased in September 1930. Goods traffic continued until the station closed entirely in July 1965.

8. Egginton Junction was a jointly-owned station situated at the point where the Great Northern and North Staffordshire Railways' routes from Derby converged. It was opened on 1st July 1878 and replaced an earlier station of the latter company situated ¼ mile to the east. Services using GNR platforms were withdrawn in 1939 and those using the NSR platforms in 1962. The rural nature of its location is obvious on this postcard.

9. Etwall, one stop nearer Derby (Friargate) on the Great Northern line, opened in April 1878 and had a regular and busy passenger service in the early years of this century. Despite this, closure to passengers came in December 1939, though goods traffic continued until 1968.

G.N.R. STATION, ILKESTON.

ILKESTON

10. The Great Northern railway station at **Ilkeston,** one of three stations at one time in the town, pictured on a card in Bestwick's series, Ilkeston, about 1912. It was on the cross-country line from Grantham to Stafford via Nottingham Victoria, and a branch line took passengers from here to Heanor via Marlpool. The station closed to passengers in September 1964, and to goods trains four years later.

11. The next station up the line from Etwall was **Mickleover** (for Radbourn), opened in 1878 and which lost its passenger trains at the same time as Etwall. Goods traffic stopped in February 1964.

CROSSHILL AND CODNOR STATION.

12. A classic case of over-enthusiastic building was the Midland Railway's line between Langley Mill and Butterley. On this postcard in the B.S.R. series, a three-coach train has just unloaded a passenger at the intermediate **Crosshill & Codnor.** This station did not open until June 1890. It was closed as a wartime economy measure between January 1917 and May 1920, and finally succumbed to road competition in May 1926.

13. Passengers from **Ripley** could travel the ten miles to Derby via Coxbench in half-an-hour in Edwardian days, when this card was published. The station was also on the Midland's Langley Mill-Butterley route. Passenger traffic stopped in June 1930.

14. Trains from **Butterley** went to Pye Bridge, Ambergate and Langley Mill on Midland Railway routes. This deserted scene is from a c.1912 card.

15. An impressive scene at **Butterley** in the early 1920s, with an Ambergate-bound service in the platform. Regular passenger services ceased in 1947. Goods traffic continued until 1964, as did occasional excursions. The station is once again in use as

the main centre of the Midland Railway Trust, a thriving preserved railway where crowded platforms are once again the norm.

16. Coxbench station was five miles from Derby on the line to Ripley. In Edwardian days, eight passenger trains stopped daily in each direction, but the service stopped in 1930. Coxbench was used for occasional excursions for a few years after regular services ceased. Goods trains used the station until 1957.

3274   MIDLAND RAILWAY STATION, DUFFIELD.

17. Duffield station is on the Midland main line from Derby north to Sheffield and Leeds, and trains on the successful line to Matlock run through it. The station seen on this W.H. Smith postcard, published about 1908, was opened in 1867 at the same time as a branch to Wirksworth and replaced an earlier structure to the north. The Wirksworth branch lost its passenger services in 1947.

18. Belper, situated to the north of Duffield, was also re-sited – this time in 1878. The present day station, seen here on a postcard from c.1910, shows a busy scene with stopping trains in each direction. Note the carefully-tended flower beds on the right and the milk churns.

19. Ambergate's distinctive triangular station dates from 1876, and was in fact the third station to open at this location. The route curving to the top left of the card ran to Manchester, while the one in the foreground was for services to Chesterfield and Butterley. Only the platform on the former Manchester route is now used, the service just operating to Matlock.

20. Whatstandwell station in all its glory about 1906. It opened in November 1894, replacing an earlier structure at the far end of the tunnel in the centre of the card. This station was named Whatstandwell Bridge, as was the present day one during its first two years of existence.

21. Matlock Bath, with an express from Manchester speeding south early this century. For over a century, crack expresses roared through here en route for the North-West. The buildings on the left are on the site of what is now a car park, catering for the machines that eroded the railway's viability. The station closed in March 1967, but was re-opened as an unstaffed halt in May 1972.

22. The austere buildings at **Darley Dale,** the first station north of Matlock. The last B.R. passenger train stopped here on 4th March 1967, but the preservation society, Peak Rail, has run trains on this stretch of line since December 1991.

23. Rowsley decorated in all its finery in 1906 for a royal visit. King Edward VII visited Chatsworth in the New Year on an annual basis. An anonymously-published card.

24. At the heart of the Peak District, **Miller's Dale** statio capable of dealing with lots of goods traffic. A large numb stop daily in the Edwardian era (Miller's Dale was the ju enlivened the atmosphere. Goods traffic was mainly lime

five platforms after track widening c.1906, and was
nger trains – 14 in each direction – were scheduled to
e branch to Buxton), while other non-stop expresses
action stopped, however, in March 1967.

25. Back south again, **Bakewell's** days as part of the British Rail network also came to an end in 1967. It had opened in August 1862, when the line was extended from Rowsley to Hassop. Interestingly, Bakewell station – and the line itself – was not included in the original Beeching Report.

26. Great Longstone (for Ashford) was originally simply called Longstone. Like many village stations, it was some way from the communities it served and might easily have been closed earlier than September 1962. Now the trackbed is part of a footpath/cycleway from Bakewell northwards.

27. Ten miles and three stations north from Millers Dale, **Chinley** was reached, where the main line through the Peak joined the Hope Valley line from Sheffield. The latter route has survived.

28. What in 1897 became the Great Central station at **New Mills** opened on 1st July 1865, and four years later came under the joint ownership of the Manchester, Sheffield & Lincolnshire Railway and the Midland. The latter continued to share the building for its branch to Hayfield until this closed in January 1970.

29. Rural **Edale** station, six miles from Chinley going east on the Hope Valley line has survived because the route is an important cross-Pennine link; the village itself is a popular spot with ramblers.

30. Hope station, one stop towards Sheffield. Ten passenger trains a day in each direction stopped in 1910.

31. A well-filled platform at **Bamford** on Market Day, Thursday, when an extra train was put on by the Midland in the early afternoon. This Edwardian card shows a view looking towards Sheffield. The signalbox is now on Peak Rail's Darley Dale station.

Grindleford Station Platform

32. Grindleford, another popular station with walkers, looking towards Manchester. Set at the entrance to Totley tunnel, at the other end of which trains emerge at Dore and Totley station, Grindleford has featured on many postcard views. At the time of this c.1906 photo, it had wooden platforms, as Hathersage does to this day.

33. Killamarsh, on the Great Central main line, and the station immediately south of Beighton *(see illus. 49).* Originally, this line was the former North Midland line to Masborough, and was actually the "old road", the original Midland main line to Leeds. The passenger service ended in March 1963, goods trains in June 1965.

34. The main-line Sheffield-Chesterfield route had **Dronfield** as its biggest intermediate station, but despite serving a large community, it closed in 1967, though was used for excursions for some time after closure. Then, after a temporary five-day re-opening in 1979 as a result of a strike by road gritters, it was permanently re-opened in January 1981.

35. Sheepbridge and Brimington, on the Great Central between Chesterfield and Staveley, closed in January 1956. This line merely duplicated a similar Midland route.

36. Chesterfield Midland is the only one of the three stations in the town still open. This W.H. Smith postcard shows the interior as it was about 1908. Note the milk churns on the platform, a common sight on stations for decades.

37. C.H. Nadin, a local Chesterfield postcard publisher, photographed the town extensively, including this card of the Midland station exterior in the days of Hansom cabs.

38. Clay Cross, where the main lines from Nottingham and Derby to Sheffield joined. It closed to passengers in January 1967, goods traffic having ceased to use the station almost three years earlier. The main station buildings are out of view to the left of the picture.

39. Doe Hill, one station south from Clay Cross on the line to Pye Bridge and Nottingham, was closed in September 1960. The photographer here seems to have specially posed a group of emerging passengers in a c.1910 scene.

WESTHOUSES AND BLACKWELL STATION.

40. Westhouses and Blackwell also principally served a mining community. It was a busy station, receiving some thirty trains a day before the First World War.

41. Passenger services at **Glapwell** survived only until July 1930. On a Midland branch between Pleasley and Staveley, it had little chance of making money for the company. With few passengers using the trains, Glapwell nevertheless had a staff of four when this photo was taken for a postcard about 1912.

42. Clown (Midland), also known from 1951 as Clowne and Barlborough, was one of two stations situated adjacent to each other serving the village. This one was on the Chesterfield-Sheffield line, and closed in July 1954. It was originally called 'Clown', and the spelling on this c.1910 postcard is incorrect.

43. The Midland's line between Mansfield and Worksop, 15 miles long, had five intermediate stations, including **Whitwell,** and a ten-train-a-day service in each direction in 1910. It was closed in October 1964. This c.1908 card was published by the prolific Worksop firm of Taylor.

44. Shirebrook Midland Station on a wet day in the first decade of this century. This was opened in June 1875 and closed on 12th October 1964. It was renamed Shirebrook West in June 1951 (though it was situated at the *east* end of the town!).

45. Market Place station in **Chesterfield** was part of a grandiose plan by the Lancashire, Derbyshire & East Coast Railway to build a major cross-country route. In fact, the line got no further than Chesterfield to Lincoln. This postcard showing Market Place exterior was published by Nadin.

46. Another Nadin card, showing Market Place interior, which closed to passengers in December 1951. Originally called simply 'Chesterfield', the suffix 'Market Place' was added when the Great Central took it over in 1907 to distinguish it from the company's other station in the town.

47. The Great Central's original **Chesterfield** station provided the town with access to what was theoretically the most direct route to London, though in practice most of the services on the Great Central main line were locals to Sheffield or Nottingham. Closure came in March 1963.

48. A superb postcard from 1911 showing the stationmaster at **Scarcliffe** posing with his family. On the Chesterfield-Langwith Junction section of the line to Lincoln, Scarcliffe was never likely to attract enough passenger traffic to justify its existence, though the goods revenue generated would have maintained the station's usefulness. Even in 1910 only four passenger trains stopped on weekdays in each direction, and the inevitable closure arrived in September 1951.

49. The magnificent Great Central station at **Beighton**, south of Sheffield, on the company's prestigious main line. In this c.1908 picture, passengers are well outnumbered by staff though, to be fair, most pictures of station staff were taken well before trains were due! It was in service for only just over half a century (replacing an earlier one) and was closed in November 1954.

50. The station provision at **Langwith Junction** was sumptuous, given the fairly low number of passenger trains: on a normal weekday there were five trains to Sheffield/ Mansfield and four to Chesterfield in 1910. Later renamed Shirebrook North, it was closed to passenger traffic in September 1955 and goods trains in January 1965. The trains must actually have been well-used, for Langwith boasted a refreshment room at one time.

51. Back on the G.C. main line, this card by A. Rippon of Chesterfield features **Heath** station, south of Chesterfield, which had a generous stopping service, given the size of the community it served, until it closed in 1963.

52. Next stop down the line to Nottingham was **Pilsley,** the exterior of which is seen here on a postcard used in September 1913.

53. Pilsley interior, which again had a good allocation of buildings. The station closed in November 1959.

54. Tibshelf Town, one of two stations serving the village. This Great Central one closed in 1963, though the Midland station had lost passenger trains in 1930.

55. The **Great Central** station at **Clowne,** originally opened by the Lancashire, Derbyshire & East Coast Railway in 1897. It hosted a mere six passenger trains each way daily, but goods provision was extensive. Stopping services ceased for ever in September 1939, but Clowne remained in use for goods traffic until July 1960. It had been renamed Clowne South in June 1951.